THE DEAD SEA SCROLLS

ELECTRONIC REFERENCE LIBRARY, 2

INCLUDING

**THE DEAD SEA SCROLLS DATABASE (NON-BIBLICAL TEXTS)
EDITED BY EMANUEL TOV**

Prepared by the Foundation for Ancient Research
and Mormon Studies and its Center for the
Preservation of Ancient Religious Texts at Brigham
Young University, Provo, Utah

Noel B. Reynolds, Producer • Donald W. Parry, Co-Director
E. Jan Wilson, Co-Director • Terrence L. Szink, Advisor

BRILL

ISBN 90 04 10891 2 (Single User)
ISBN 90 04 10892 0 (Multi User)

Printed in The Netherlands

CONTENTS

ACKNOWLEDGMENTS

The Foundation for Ancient Research and Mormon Studies (FARMS) began work on producing an electronic version of the Dead Sea Scrolls in 1992. The FARMS team at that time consisted of Noel B. Reynolds, Professor of Political Science, Brigham Young University (BYU) and then President of FARMS, Donald W. Parry, Associate Professor of Hebrew Language and Literature, BYU, and Steven W. Booras, Technical Operations Manager at FARMS. Subsequently, E. Jan Wilson, Associate Director of the Center for the Preservation of Ancient Religious Texts, Monte F. Shelley, Director of Instructional Applications Services, BYU, and James S. Rosenvall, Manager of the WordCruncher Development Team, BYU, joined the team. The original idea for the database was provided by Emanuel Tov of the Hebrew University, who also supervised the final phase of the project, involving the proofreading of the data in Jerusalem and the final decisions concerning the scope of the database. Data were entered over the years by Terry Szink, Kerry Muhlestein, Jan Wilson, David Geilman, Irena Abramian, and Richard Wilson. The images were scanned and prepared for electronic publication by Eileen Wilson and Cindy Booras. The database was eventually completed by The Center for the Preservation of Ancient Religious Texts (CPART), a department of FARMS, and the texts were proofread in Jerusalem under the supervision of Emanuel Tov in June-July 1999 by Ayelet Tov-Sagi. The technical part of the User's Manual was rewritten in September 1999 by Michaël N. van der Meer, with advice from Aernold van Gosliga, on the basis of earlier formulations by FARMS. FARMS is grateful to these individuals for their fine contributions to this project.

We also appreciate the collaborative efforts of Weston W. Fields, Executive Director of the Dead Sea Scrolls Foundation, Daniel C. Peterson, Director of CPART, and Daniel Oswald, Executive Director of FARMS and Hans van der Meij, Senior Acquisitions Editor of Brill Academic Publishers. Thanks are expressed to James A. Sanders, President, and Michael Phelps, Executive Director, of the Ancient Biblical Manuscript Center, Claremont, CA, for the scroll/fragment photographs. FARMS is also indebted to the advisors to the project–Weston Fields, Florentino García Martínez, Dana M. Pike, Elisha Qimron, Lawrence H. Schiffman, David R. Seely, Shemaryahu Talmon, Emanuel Tov, and Eugene Ulrich–for their expert advice and professional encouragement.

FARMS also wishes to express its gratitude to Alan and Karen Ashton and to anonymous donors whose generosity made this project possible.

Foundation for Ancient Research and Mormon Studies at
Brigham Young University, Provo, Utah

I

BRIEF DESCRIPTION OF THE DEAD SEA SCROLLS ELECTRONIC REFERENCE LIBRARY (NON-BIBLICAL TEXTS)

A   INTRODUCTION

A major purpose of creating the database was to put in the hands of scholars a tool that would allow them to do sophisticated electronic searches on the Dead Sea Scrolls texts in ways that would facilitate their study of the scroll material and in this way advance scholarship in that area. At the same time, the database was created in a flexible way, so as to enable further products or ways of research at a later stage. To further enhance the database, images of the scrolls were appended to each document or group of documents allowing the users to decide on questionable readings by examining the images themselves.

Other files in the database contain the Hebrew Bible, the Septuagint (edition of Rahlfs), the Vulgate, and the King James Version, as well as the English translations of the Dead Sea Scrolls published in *The Dead Sea Scrolls Translated* by F. García Martínez (Second Edition; Leiden: Brill, 1996).

B   COVERAGE OF THE DATABASE

The database covers all non-biblical Hebrew, Aramaic, Nabatean, and Greek texts from Qumran and a selection of texts from Wadi Murabba'at and Naḥal Ḥever. For an exact list of the texts included, see the list of texts within the database.

The following texts are *excluded* from the present database:

a   All the texts from Wadi Daliyeh, Khirbet Mird, Jericho, Wadi Nar, Naḥal Mishmar, Wadi Sdeir (Naḥal David), Wadi Ghweir, and Masada.

b   All the biblical texts, Phylacteries (*tefillin*) and *Mezuzot* from Qumran and other sites (in this definition, the term 'biblical' is taken in a wide sense, so that the Ben Sira texts are excluded as well). According to the aforementioned understanding of the nature of the FARMS database, at present the *Psalms Scroll* from Cave 11 (11QPs^a) is excluded, since this scroll has been published in *DJD* IV as a regular biblical text. However, at a next stage, the noncanonical segments of this scroll, as well as of 4QPs^{e,f} and 11QPs^b, will probably be included in the database.

c   Texts which are not yet ready for inclusion in the database (see the Appendix).

d   Texts which are too fragmentary for inclusion in the database, such as 1Q48, 1Q59-61, 2QX1.

e   Texts which are mere names in the inventory list: Although listed in the earlier inventory of J. Milik, these texts have not been identified on the photographs (such as 4Q229-233).

C   TEXTS

C.1   STRUCTURE OF THE DATABASE

The texts included in the database are subdivided according to archaeological sites: Qumran (further subdivided by cave), Murabba'at, etc. Within each site or cave the texts are arranged sequentially by inventory number. An additional criterion for subdivision in the database pertains to the languages of the texts (Hebrew, Aramaic/Nabatean, Greek/Latin), so as to enable word searches in these languages.

C.2   EDITIONS USED

The following editions were used for the database:
a   The main source for the database was the transcriptions included in the *DJD* series: *Discoveries in the Judaean Desert [of Jordan]* I –, published by Oxford University Press, Oxford from 1955 onwards. The following volumes are covered: I, II, III, V, VI, VII, VIII, IX, X, XI, XIII, XVIII, XIX, XX, XXI (most texts), XXII, XXIII, XXV, XXVI, XXVII, XXIX, XXXIV, XXXV, XXXVI (most texts). Although almost all texts of the corpora from Qumran, Wadi Murabba'at, and Naḥal Ḥever are included, coverage is incomplete, since as of August 1999 not all texts from these sites have been published in or finalized for the *DJD* series. The texts not presented in the database are listed in the Appendix.
b   11QT^a (11Q19, the main copy of the Temple Scroll) is recorded according to the edition of E. Qimron. Since this edition covers also 11Q20, 4Q365a and 4Q524, the *DJD* editions of these texts are excluded from the database.
c   1QapGen, 1QpHab, 1QS, 1QM, 1QH^a, 4Q201-208 are recorded according to the edition of E. J. C. Tigchelaar and F. García Martínez, *The Dead Sea Scrolls Study Edition* (Volumes I & II; Leiden/New York/Köln: Brill, 1997-1998). The texts from Cave 1 have not been included in *DJD*, and likewise 4Q201-208 were initially not included either in *DJD*, although 4Q201, 203, 206, 208-209 are included in vol. XXVI.
All editions are used with permission.
  A detailed list of the texts included in the database may be viewed in the database itself, as the file/book "Contents of the DSS Database."

C.3   RE-EDITIONS

As a rule, *DJD* does not contain re-editions. The six re-editions included in the later volumes of the series are not recorded at this stage.

The texts recorded reflect as precisely as possible the editions consulted, and these editions, in their turn, reflect the fragments themselves as precisely as possible.

a   *The structure of individual columns of the text within the composition, extant or reconstructed, often based on physically unconnected fragments placed in an extant or reconstructed column sequence.* Some scholars made more suggestions than others regarding the reconstruction of the column structure of the scroll on the basis of the preserved fragments. Extant and reconstructed columns are numbered with large Roman numerals (I, II, etc.). Columns are presented sequentially and when the remains of one of the two columns are very scanty, they are often represented next to each other. Different columns found in a single fragment are also numbered with lower-case Roman numerals (e.g., frag. 1 i 8). Usually the numbering starts with the first preserved column, although some scholars also take into consideration columns they presume to have preceded those that have been preserved. The (preserved) fragments comprising each column are numbered a, b, c, etc.; unconnected fragments are numbered 1, 2, 3, etc. (sometimes subdivided into 1a, 1b, etc.). The lines of each column are numbered 1, 2, 3, etc., starting with the first preserved line. In some cases, when there is certainty about the number of lines preceding the first preserved line-especially when one or more adjacent columns are preserved-the first preserved line may be numbered with a later number. Some scholars, preferring to retain the number '1' for the first preserved line, number the presumed, preceding lines as 01, 02, etc.

b   *Indication of top and bottom margins, when extant.* Top and bottom margins, when (partially) preserved, are always indicated. Left and right margins are not indicated explicitly, since the lack of square brackets at the right and left indicates the existence of such margins. In vol. VIII, however, such margins are indicated explicitly.

c   *Spaces within the text, as well as completely empty lines.* Within the text spaces are indicated by *vac(at)* at the beginning of the line (indentations), in the middle, or at the end of the lines. Stretches which are not inscribed as a result of rough material or damage to the leather are indicated in some volumes by *vac(at)* and in others by ///. Completely empty lines are numbered.

d   *Opisthographs. Recto* and *verso* are indicated, as well as the 'lower' and 'upper' versions in the documentary texts in vol. XXVII.

e   *The exact position of the letters in the columns and fragments.* While an attempt was made to imitate the position of the letters in the fragments, often the printed text can merely approximate the fragments, because printed and written letters have different widths; moreover, while printed letter-widths are consistent, hand-written letter-widths vary, even if only slightly. Some editors occasionally left double spaces between words in order to compensate for the limitations of the printed layout.

f   *Supralinear, infralinear, and (less frequent) marginal additions* are indicated in the text by raised characters (often in a smaller font), or when longer than one word, often by an additional line, which sometimes is indicated with a special number (line 9a would indicate a supralinear addition above line 9). Sometimes, the exact position of the supralinear letter or word cannot be indicated accurately.

g   *Dots between words in the palaeo-Hebrew script, letters or words written in the palaeo-Hebrew script, numbers, etc.*

h   *Various types of corrections and erasures*: erasures of the leather or papyrus, indicated by { }; the crossing out of a word or line: את; deletion dots above, below, or around the letters. Earlier volumes of *DJD* did not differentiate among the different types of deletions, representing them all uniformly by {{ }}.

i   *Letters omitted by scribes and 'superfluous letters'* are sometimes indicated in the earlier volumes by < > or ( ), with the missing letters added into the transcription, and { }, respectively.

j   *Various degrees of certainty regarding the reconstruction of letters, based on the subjective assessment of each editor's evaluation of the preserved state of the letters.* Usually, a probable letter is denoted by a dot above it (e.g. א̇), a possible letter is denoted by a circlet above it (e.g. א̊), and a remnant of an unidentified letter is represented by a mid-line circlet (e.g. ○). In a few *DJD* volumes (especially vols. x and xxxiv) the uncertainty concerning the distinction between *waw* and *yod* as well as between final and non-final *mem* is indicated by a *macron*, and in the present database this *macron* is represented with a dot. Different possibilities of letters are sometimes recorded in *DJD* by stacking letters above each other, especially in vol. xxvii. In Greek texts, Greek papyrological conventions are followed, including the placing of dots under the letters.

k   *Reconstructions* are enclosed in square brackets. Left brackets at the end of the line are often omitted when the length of the line is unclear. Right brackets at the beginning of the line are usually provided, but they are not found in vol. xxv. Search programs used in the database often required the addition of square brackets at the beginning or end of the line when these brackets are not used in the *DJD* editions themselves.

Texts which have been entered on the basis of the edition of E. J. C. Tigchelaar and F. García Martínez, *Study Edition* (1QapGen, 1QpHab, 1QS, 1QM, 1QH^a, 4Q201-208) do not denote questionable letters in accord with the procedure followed in that edition.

C.5 NAMES OF THE COMPOSITIONS

The names of the compositions in the database follow the conventions of *DJD* and in the case of French names they are translated into English. These names were updated according to E. Tov, 'A List of the Texts from the Judaean Desert,' in: P. W. Flint and J. C. VanderKam (eds.), *The Dead Sea Scrolls after Fifty Years-A Comprehensive Assessment* (Volume II; Leiden/Boston/Köln: Brill, 1999: 669-717) and beyond this list according to the most updated names as recorded in the files of the *Dead Sea Scrolls Publication Project*, Jerusalem.

D IMAGES

Each text or part of a text (a column) is accompanied by an icon of an image of the text which becomes visible when selected. These images display either only the text or column in question or the PAM (Palestine Archaeological Museum) plate containing the selected text together with other texts.

The following sources were consulted for the identification and selection of the images from the available sources: S. Reed, *The Dead Sea Scrolls Catalogue, Documents, Photographs and Museum Inventory Numbers* (SBL Resources for Biblical Study 32; Atlanta, GA 1994); E. Tov with the collaboration of S. J. Pfann, *The Dead Sea Scrolls on Microfiche-A Comprehensive Facsimile Edition of the Texts from the Judean Desert*, with a *Companion Volume* (Leiden: Brill and IDC, 1993); id., *Companion Volume to The Dead Sea Scrolls Microfiche Edition* (Second Revised Edition; Leiden: Brill and IDC, 1995). In each case only one image was selected for inclusion in the database. Usually the most recent photos were chosen, generally from the 44.000 and 43.000 series of the Palestine Archaeological Museum. For further images of the same document, see the lists in the aforementioned inventories by Tov and Pfann.

A second criterion for the selection of images was that of clarity: earlier negatives which were clearer than later ones were sometimes preferred. On a selected number of images, some minor, low level enhancement was applied to adjust brightness and contrast. The arrangement of the fragments on the plates was not changed. The electronic images were obtained from negatives in possession of the Ancient Biblical Manuscript Center in Claremont, California (Michael Phelps, Director), with a few additional images from the John Trever collection.

E WORD SEARCHES

Within the database the texts are arranged according to their sequence in the inventory of the texts (that is, for example, 4Q250, 4Q251, etc.), tagged according to their language (Hebrew, Aramaic/Nabatean, Greek/Latin). Within the SearchManager, searches are performed according to these languages, so that in any given instance all relevant words can be called up, for example, in the texts of Cave 1 or of all the caves. Searches can be performed for individual words, or entire phrases using the SearchManager. Wild card searches are also possible, and this feature is helpful for scholars working with fragments that only contain parts of words. The SearchManager allows the user to place segments of words within a known context. Searches can also be performed to locate words within a given proximity to other words, and in relation to this, it is even possible to do collocation analyses.

The Hebrew and Aramaic "internal" lexicons may be used to perform searches on roots of the words included in each lexicon as well as on the inflected forms of those roots (in Hebrew, e.g., all forms belonging to the *halakh* word group). One may also use the internal lexicons to search for certain grammatical forms of a given root (e.g. all the *hithpa'el* forms of a given verb).

Knowledge of the idiosyncracies of the Qumran orthography and morphology is not always necessary, since most related words are grouped together in the lexicon. Thus the different forms of מאד (that is, including מאדה, מאוד, מאודה, and מואדה) are listed under the heading of מאד, and with the use of the Lexicon Dialog Box they can be called up together. For a detailed description of the nature and possibilities of the search procedures, see the help-files in the database itself, and sections II-VI below. The Greek search is not based on a lexicon, and is therefore more limited.

F   AREAS FOR FUTURE IMPROVEMENT

1   While the great majority of the images reflect their accompanying texts in all their details, further research is needed to examine the compatibility between the two. In some cases additional images are needed.

2   The texts which have been entered on the basis of E. J. C. Tigchelaar and F. García Martínez, *Study Edition*, and which therefore do not denote questionable letters with diacritical signs will be recorded differently.

3   The internal lexicon indicating the roots, inflected forms and a grammatical analysis, has been kindly provided by Professors Alan Groves and Steve Vanderhill who have allowed us to use their database as a basis for the word searches in the present program. It must be noted that several words in the Dead Sea Scrolls do not appear in the Westminster database, because that database was based on the Hebrew Bible, although some of them have been added. The search facilities are therefore included for the convenience of the user without any claim to completeness. Moreover, the morphological analyses for all forms are based on the Westminster analyses and were not reviewed at FARMS except for some global changes in terminology. The next version of the present database will insert necessary corrections in the lexicon and morphological analysis.

4   The next version will complete the coverage of the texts from Judean Desert. For a list of the texts not covered by present database, see above and the Appendix.

5   In principle the spacing and layout of the texts have been adapted to that in the editions. However, due to time limitations, only two thirds of this work was finished. While the text in one third of the texts is identical with that of the *DJD* editions, and word searches may be conducted, in some cases long spaces in the texts are recorded in the present database as smaller spaces.

6   The various manuscripts of the Temple Scroll (11Q19, 11Q20, 4Q365a and 4Q524) will be recorded differently in the future.

APPENDIX
TEXTS EXCLUDED FROM THE DATABASE

Three texts are included in the database, not as separate texts,
but as part of Qimron's edition of 11Q19, 11Q20, 4Q365a, and 4Q524.
The following Qumran texts, several of which are now ready, are *not*
included in the version of August 1999 (slight fluctuations in the names
are possible).

4Q238	Hab 3 (temporary name)
4Q249a	pap cryptA Serekh ha-'Edah[a]
4Q249b	pap cryptA Serekh ha-'Edah[b]
4Q249c	pap cryptA Serekh ha-'Edah[c]
4Q249d	pap cryptA Serekh ha-'Edah[d]
4Q249e	pap cryptA Serekh ha-'Edah[e]
4Q249f	pap cryptA Serekh ha-'Edah[f]
4Q249g	pap cryptA Serekh ha-'Edah[g]
4Q249h	pap cryptA Serekh ha-'Edah[h]
4Q249i	pap cryptA Serekh ha-'Edah[i]
4Q249j	pap cryptA Lev[h]?
4Q249k	pap cryptA Text Quoting Leviticus A
4Q249l	pap cryptA Text Quoting Leviticus B
4Q249m	pap cryptA Hodayot-like Text D
4Q249n	pap cryptA Liturgical Work E?
4Q249o	pap cryptA Liturgical Work F?
4Q249p	pap cryptA Prophecy?
4Q249q	pap cryptA Frag. Mentioning Planting
4Q249r	pap cryptA Unid. Text A
4Q249s	pap cryptA Unid. Text B
4Q249t	pap cryptA Unid. Text C
4Q249u	pap cryptA Unid. Text D
4Q249v	pap cryptA Unid. Text E
4Q249w	pap cryptA Unid. Text F
4Q249x	pap cryptA Unid. Text G
4Q249y	pap cryptA Unid. Text H
4Q249z	pap cryptA Miscellaneous Frags.
4Q250	pap cryptA Text Concerning Cultic Service A
4Q250a	pap cryptA Text Concerning Cultic Service B (r + v)
4Q250b	pap cryptA Text Related to Isa 11 (r + v)
4Q250c	pap cryptA Unid. Text J (recto of 4Q250d)
4Q250d	pap cryptA Unid. Text K (verso of 4Q250c)
4Q250e	pap cryptA Unid. Text L (recto of 4Q250f)
4Q250f	pap cryptA Unid. Text M (verso of 4Q250e)
4Q250g	pap cryptA Unid. Text N (r+v)
4Q250h	pap cryptA Unid. Text O (r+v)
4Q250i	pap cryptA Unid. Text P (r+v)
4Q250j	pap cryptA Misc. Texts (r+v)
4Q285	Sefer ha-Milhamah
4Q313	cryptA Miqsat Ma'aseh ha-Torah[g]?
4Q313a	cryptA Cal. Doc. E
4Q313b	cryptA Unid. Text Q
4Q313c	cryptA Unid. Text R

4Q319	Otot (*olim* 4QS^b + 4QS^e; 4Q260b)
4Q320	Cal. Doc. Mishmarot A (*olim* Mishmarot A)
4Q324c	cryptA Cal. Doc. B
4Q332a	Historical Text F?
4Q337	Cal. Doc. F
4Q362	cryptB undeciphered frags. A
4Q363	cryptB undeciphered frags. B
4Q363a	cryptC Text
4Q368	apocrPent. A
4Q371	apocrJoseph^a
4Q372	apocrJoseph^b
4Q373	apocrJoseph^c
4Q377	apocrPent. B (*olim* apocrMoses C)
4Q383	apocrJer A
4Q385	psEzek^a
4Q385a	Jer C^a (*olim* psMos^a)
4Q385b	psEzek^c (*olim* 4Q385 frag. 24, apocr Jer C)
4Q386	psEzek^b
4Q387a	Jer C^b (*olim* psMos^b)
4Q387b	apocrJer D
4Q388	psEzek^d
4Q388a	Jer C^c (*olim* psMos^c)
4Q389	Jer C^d (*olim* psMos^d)
4Q389a	Jer E (*olim* apocrMos^e)
4Q390	psMos^e
4Q419	Sap. Work B
4Q440a	Hodayot-like Text D
4Q440b	Fragment Mentioning a Court
4Q458	Narrative A
4Q465	papText Mentioning Samson?
4Q469	Narrative I
4Q529	Words of Michael ar
4Q530	EnGiants^b ar
4Q531	EnGiants^c ar
4Q532	EnGiants^d ar
4Q533	EnGiants^e ar (Eschat. Vision?)
4Q534	Birth of Noah^a ar (*olim* Elect of God ar)
4Q535	Birth of Noah^b (*olim* Aramaic N)
4Q536	Birth of Noah^c (*olim* Aramaic C)
4Q537	TJacob? ar
4Q538	TJud ar
4Q539	TJoseph ar (*olim* aJo ar)
4Q540	apocrLevi^a? ar (*olim* AhA [bis] = TLevi^g? ar)
4Q541	apocrLevi^b? ar (*olim* AhA = TLevi^h? ar)
4Q542	TQahat ar
4Q543	Visions of Amram^a ar
4Q544	Visions of Amram^b ar
4Q545	Visions of Amram^c ar
4Q546	Visions of Amram^d ar
4Q547	Visions of Amram^e ar
4Q548	Visions of Amram^f ar

4Q549	Visions of Amram^g? ar (*olim* Work Mentioning Hur and Miriam ar)
4Q550	PrEsther^a ar
4Q550a	PrEsther^b ar
4Q550b	PrEsther^c ar
4Q550c	PrEsther^d ar
4Q550d	PrEsther^e ar
4Q550e	PrEsther^f ar
4Q551	DanSuz? ar
4Q552	Four Kingdoms^a ar
4Q553	Four Kingdoms^b ar
4Q554	NJ^a ar
4Q555	NJ^b ar
4Q556	Vision^a ar
4Q557	Vision^c ar
4Q558	papVision^b ar
4Q559	papBibChronology ar
4Q560	Exorcism ar
4Q561	Physiognomy/Horoscope ar
4Q562	Aramaic D
4Q563	Aramaic E
4Q564	Aramaic F
4Q565	Aramaic G
4Q566	Aramaic H
4Q567	Aramaic I
4Q568	Aramaic K
4Q569	Aramaic L
4Q570	Aramaic R
4Q571	Aramaic V
4Q572	Aramaic W
4Q573	Aramaic X
4Q574	Aramaic Y
4Q575	Aramaic Z

II

GETTING STARTED

II. 1 SYSTEM REQUIREMENTS

The present Dead Sea Scrolls Electronic Reference Library is designed
for optimal performance under
- Windows 9x/NT on a Pentium 166 (or higher)
- 32 MB RAM
- SVGA 800 x 600
- 32x CD-ROM player

Minimal configuration
- Windows 3.11 on a 486
- 8 MB RAM
- VGA 640 x 480
- 4x CD-ROM player

Note: DSS Electronic Reference Library has also been successfully tested
running under Virtual PC on the Macintosh platform.

II.2 INSTALLATION

Open Windows as usual and insert the CD-ROM into your CD-ROM drive.

Windows 9x/NT
- Click the START button and select RUN
- Type:
  D:\SETUP (or E:\SETUP in case E:\ is the letter of your CD-ROM
  player)
- Follow the instructions given by the installation program

Windows 3.11
- Select RUN ... from the FILE menu
- Type into the command line field:
  D:\SETUP (or E:\SETUP in case E:\ is the letter of your CD-
  ROM player)
- Follow the instructions given by the installation program

Please note:
- The installation program asks whether you want to install either
  the Standard Israeli keyboard or the Hebrew-QWERTY keyboard as
  standard keyboard. Western scholars will probably prefer the
  Hebrew-QWERTY keyboard.

II.3 UNINSTALL

The software can be removed from your computer via the uninstall procedure under Windows:

Windows 9x/NT
- Open Windows
- Choose CONFIGURATION
- Choose SOFTWARE
- Select Dead Sea Scrolls Reference Library
- Choose DELETE

Windows 3.11
- Click on the Icon Dead Sea Scrolls Electronic Reference Library
- Choose DELETE from the FILE menu
- Confirm the choice by pressing the Yes button

II.4 STARTING THE SOFTWARE

Windows 9x/NT
- Click on the Icon START in the Windows screen
- Select PROGRAMS
- Select DSS Electronic Reference Library
- Click on DSS Electronic Reference Library

Windows 3.11
- Click on the Icon DSS Electronic Reference Library

II.5 CLOSING THE SOFTWARE

- Click on the button with 'X' in the right-top corner of the screen or Select Exit from the Menu File

III

CONTENTS OF THE ELECTRONIC REFERENCE LIBRARY

III.1 THE LOCAL LIBRARY WINDOW

Once the program has been installed under Windows the following window appears:

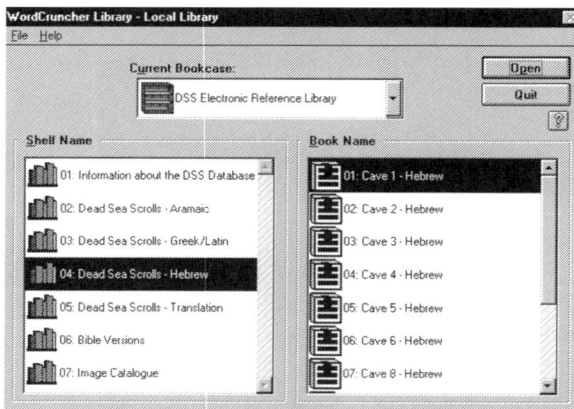

FIGURE 1
Local Library

The database is organized in shelves (left part of the screen) which are further subdivided into books (right part).

The contents of the Dead Sea Scrolls Electronic Reference Library are described in detail in Book 01 '*Introduction to the Dead Sea Scrolls Database*' of Shelf 01.

Following is a brief overview of the contents of each shelf.

Shelf 01: Information about the Dead Sea Scrolls Database
    Book 01: Introduction to the Dead Sea Scrolls Database
    Book 02: How to Use the Dead Sea Scrolls Database (an electronic
           version of this user's manual)
    Book 03: Contents of the Dead Sea Scrolls Database (a simple Table
           of Contents)

The next three shelves of the Dead Sea Scrolls are the scroll fragments themselves organized by language:
Shelf 02: Aramaic/Nabatean
Shelf 03: Greek/Latin
Shelf 04: Hebrew

Shelf 05: Dead Sea Scrolls – Translation
   1996 English translation of the non-biblical Dead Sea Scrolls by
   F. García Martínez (see Introduction).

Shelf 06: Biblical Versions
   Book 01: Hebrew Bible with unvocalized text
   Book 02: Greek Septuagint
   Book 03: Latin Vulgate version of the Old Testament
   Book 04: English King James version of the Old Testament

Shelf 07: Image Catalog
   Book 01: the catalog of Scroll images

Please note that:
- The textual basis of the 1996 English Translation by F. García Martínez differs from the Hebrew and Aramaic texts included in the present database.
- In order to open more than one shelf at the same time, another instance of the program must be opened. In order to have both the Hebrew/Aramaic text and García Martínez's 1996 English translation of the same Qumran document on the screen, one has to start the program a second time and adjust the size of the windows.

III.2 THE MENUS

The WordCruncher software enables the user to do various simple and complex searches in the database. These searches can be initiated with help of the options in the six pull down menus that appear on the top of the screen once a particular book is opened with a double click of the mouse:

File	Open Book
	Save
	Copy
	Print
	Print Setup
	Publisher Information
	Book Information
	Exit

Search	FindIt, SearchManager
	Previous line (Ctrl+Up)
	Next Line (Ctrl+Down)
	Previous Cave (Ctrl+Shift+Up)
	Next Cave (Ctrl+Shift+Down)
	Goto Previous Level (Ctrl+Shift+Home)
	Goto Next (Ctrl+Shift+End)
	Concordance / Index

View	Table of Contents
	Full Citation
	Reference List
	Previous Reference (Ctrl+PgUp)
	Next Reference (Ctrl+PgDn)
	Log
	No External Reference Works

Options	General Preferences
	Book Preferences
	Basic Menus
	Advanced Menus
	Display Language
	Keyboards
	Choice text Styles

Window	Maximize Top Window
	Cascade
	Tile
	Tile Horizontal
	Tile Vertical
	New Text Window
	Close Top Text Window (Esc)
	Close All Except Top Text Window

Help	Contents
	Index
	How to Use Help
	Coach
	About WordCruncher View

Please note that:
- These menus are part of the WordCruncher software. The information in the Help files is of a general nature and may not always provide the answers to specific questions concerning the present Dead Sea Scrolls Database.
- Some general WordCruncher options have not been implemented in this product. These options will appear grayed out on the menus.

III.3 USING THE TABLE OF CONTENTS

To go quickly to a particular text within a file, or to a particular section of a given text, use the Table of Contents in the "View" menu.

Example:
Open "Cave 1 – Hebrew" and select the "View" menu. Then select "Table of Contents." This will show some icons with small buttons to the left. If these buttons have a +, you may click on them to expand the document. In this case, click on the button beside "Cave 1" and a list of the texts in Cave 1 will be displayed, as seen in figure 2.

FIGURE 2
Using the Table of Contents

Highlight any one of these and the text window will automatically reposition itself to bring that text into the window. You may also open up further subdivisions such as fragments or columns.

As an alternative to the Table of Contents, you may right-click on any of the reference level names in the book's title bar and then double-click on one of the resulting options in the drop-down window to jump to that area of the book.

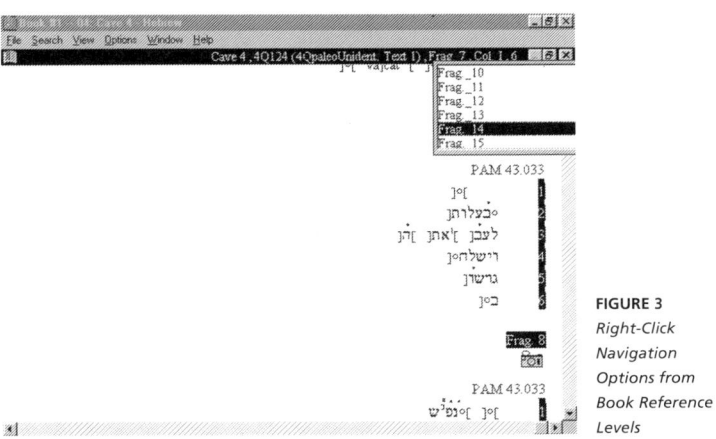

FIGURE 3
Right-Click Navigation Options from Book Reference Levels

Finally, the options in the search menu will also help to move quickly through the various books (see above section III.2).

Your location in any given document is displayed at the top of the screen. Scrolling down shows the change in location as noted in the blue bar above the text screen. You may also display the levels within the text window. Indeed, the levels may be displayed by default on your screen.

- If not, you may display them by opening the "Options" menu
- and then clicking on "Book preferences."
- After that, click the box beside "show reference codes" so that an x is displayed in that small box.
- Then click OK.

The column and line numbers will then be visible in the text window.

You may also change the zoom or the font size by selecting the size you wish within the "Book preferences" dialog box.

IV

USING THE IMAGES

A single click on any image icon within the database is sufficient to open that image (including the images contained within this instruction manual). In the case of images which contain multiple fragments, we have presented the image in its original form and not made any attempt to isolate the particular fragment associated with the text in question.

In the case of small fragments the selected fragment is presented together with the other fragments on the PAM photograph.

The images may be enlarged (zoomed) or reduced by using the scroll bar in the bottom left corner of the image window.

A portion of the image may also be enlarged simply by selecting it with the cursor and describing a rectangle over the area which is to be enlarged. To do that, click on a point in the image and hold the mouse button down while moving the cursor to another point in the image. You will see the outline of a rectangle form, and when you release the mouse button, the area within that rectangle will fill the window.

A third method for enlarging a portion of the image is to hold down the shift key. That will cause the cursor to assume the shape of a magnifying glass. If you then click anywhere in the image, it will be enlarged. By holding the shift key and the alt key at the same time, the magnifying glass will change from + to – and the image will be reduced in size when you click.

When you have finished viewing the image, close it by pressing the escape key or by clicking the Windows close button.

In conjunction with the images provided in the present database, some users may prefer to use Volume 1 of the present Dead Sea Scrolls Electronic Reference Library, edited by Timothy H. Lim in consultation with Philip S. Alexander. Published in 1997 by Oxford University Press and Brill Academic Publishers. ISBN 90-04-10697-9 (Single User) or 90-04-10788-6 (Multi User). This tool will enable the user to manipulate the brightness of the photos and to rotate the several fragments.

V
SEARCHES

V.1 SIMPLE WORD SEARCHES

If you wish to look up all occurrences of a particular word in the database, you have three choices.

The simplest method is to double-click on the word within the text. A list will be produced which contains all the occurrences of that word within the file that has been opened. The total number of hits is noted in the upper right corner, and the number of the occurrence within the list is also notes. For example 3/22 would mean the third occurrence out of a total of 22 occurrences.

Example:
In 4Q158, Frag. 1-2, the word עם appears in the fourth line. By double clicking on that word, the following list appears.

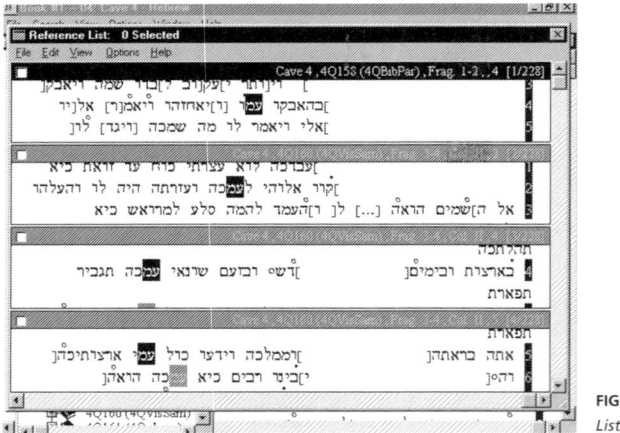

FIGURE 4
List of hits

Please note that:

- The search results may present homographs such as the nouns דָּבָר <dabar> and דֶּבֶר <deber> and the verbal form דִּבֶּר <dibber> together. The user can search for these words separately via the option Lexicon Dialog Box (see below).
- The search results present all relevant words in the database, whether they are completely preserved (e.g., כתב <katab>), only partly preserved (e.g. ב[כת] <[kat]ab>), or have been completely reconstructed (e.g. [כתב] < [katab]>).
- Several words in the Dead Sea Scrolls do not appear in the Westminster database, since that database was based on the Hebrew

Bible, although some of them have been added. The search facilities are included for the convenience of the user without any claim to completeness. Moreover, the morphological analyses for all the forms are based on the Westminster analyses and were not reviewed by FARMS (see above section I).

- As a rule, the search results will appear on the screen together with all the diacritical indications for partially preserved letters. However, in the few cases where the texts are quoted from the Dead Sea Scrolls Study Edition by F. García Martínez and E.J.C. Tigchelaar instead of the DJD edition, such diacritical indications are absent. (see above section I).

- The WordCruncher software recognizes only the words as they were written by the first hand. In the few cases of scribal corrections the user may have to perform several searches.
For example: the passages in 4Q216 where the word מלאך occurs with the aleph in supralinear position as a scribal correction, the software will recognize this list this word under מל rather than מלאך.

- Note further that the list includes forms with prefixes and suffixes. Such affixes are separated from the main word by invisible markers. Therefore, if you wish to find forms which include such affixes, you will have to use one of the other two possibilities.
See further below 'Searches involving the internal lexicon'

If you wish to search for a word that is not present on the screen, you may use "FindIt," which may be accessed from the "Search" menu. If you wish to search in Hebrew, be sure that Hebrew is the active language. If it is not, then select it from the drop-down "Search Category" menu.

Note:

Two Hebrew keyboards are available: the QWERTY keyboard (used by some western scholars) and the standard Israeli keyboard. You may change the keyboard by using the drop-down keyboard menu in the "FindIt" window, or by choosing the "show keyboard" from the "Options" menu in the "SearchManager," or by simply clicking on "keyboards" under "Options" on the main menu bar. In this last case, the keyboard will automatically appear when you open either "FindIt" or the "SearchManager." These keyboards (as well as the Greek keyboard available in Greek texts) are illustrated in Figure 5.

The most powerful search method is the "SearchManager" which may be accessed from the "Search" menu or by simply pressing "Enter." The window shown in Figure 6 will then open.

Note that there is a 'Search Category' drop-down menu at the top for language groups. If you wish to search in Hebrew and Hebrew is not displayed, then choose it from that list. The Hebrew words will then be displayed in alphabetical order, and you may select a word from the word wheel by simply scrolling the word wheel and then clicking on the button to the right of it (with the glasses icon). Alternatively, you may type in the word at the bottom (note the comment on keyboards above).

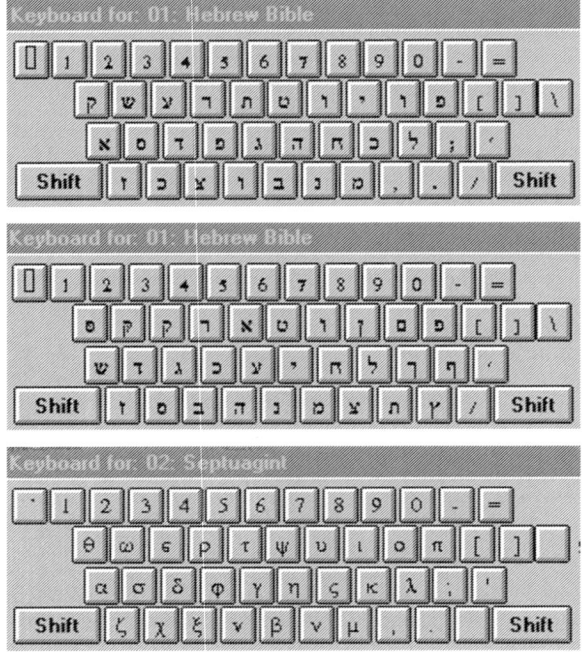

FIGURE 5
Hebrew and Greek Keyboard Layouts

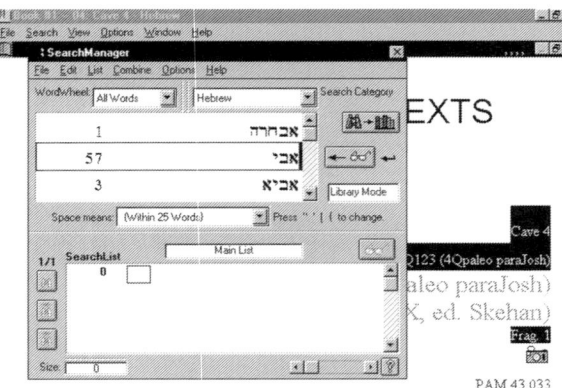

FIGURE 6
SearchManager window

V.2   SEARCHES INVOLVING THE INTERNAL LEXICONS

In the database, the normal verbal prefixes and suffixes are not separated (except for object suffixes). Therefore, if you wish to see all the forms of a particular verb root, you must use the internal lexicon. This lexicon also provides a grammatical analysis for the various inflected forms.

Example:
- Open the book "Cave 1 – Hebrew"
- and then open the SearchManager in the normal fashion.
- Type in the verb form אלך
  Do not push the "insert" key at this point, because that will insert the word אלך and rotate the WordWheel to the next word in the list and the lexicon results will be displayed for whatever word is between the guide lines on the WordWheel. Thus if you type in אלך and press the "insert" key, the lexicon results will be for the next word on the WordWheel, which is אלם.
- After typing אלך, open the "List" menu in the SearchManager.
- From the drop-down menu select "Lexicon dialog box." That will display the window shown in Figure 7.

You will notice that on the right side of this box is a list of all the inflected forms that occur within the database. There is a number associated with each form that tells you how many occurrences of each form may be found in the document currently open. There are also grammatical notations. If you wish to do searches on certain inflected forms, you may highlight those forms and search on them.

For example, if you wish to create a list of all the *hithpa'el* forms of a certain verb,
- highlight those forms (using the Control key and clicking on them),
- then click on the button labeled "combine" and you will see that the label on that button immediately changes to "use."
- Click on it again and you will have the list placed in the SearchManager.
- You may then press the "insert" key
- and click on the button in the SearchManager which will display the list of hits.

Please note that in a few cases letters like *waw* and *yod* are somewhat difficult to distinguish on the screen.

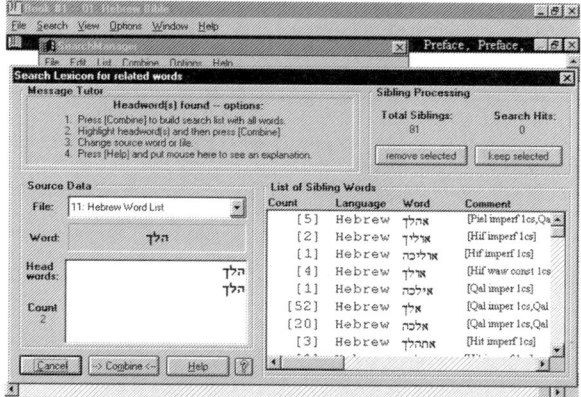

FIGURE 7

Lexicon dialog box

You can look up occurrences of a word or search string in more than one document. To do so, you must be in the "library" search mode.
- If you are in the normal search mode, you may switch to the library search mode
- by opening the "Options" menu in the SearchManager
- and clicking on "change to Library Search mode."
A small window will then appear to the right of the WordWheel with the label "Library mode."

Example:
- After you have selected the library search mode,
- type in the word מקדש
- and press the "insert" button.
- Then click on the button in the upper right corner of the SearchManager which has the icon showing binoculars and an arrow pointing to books.
This will open the following window:

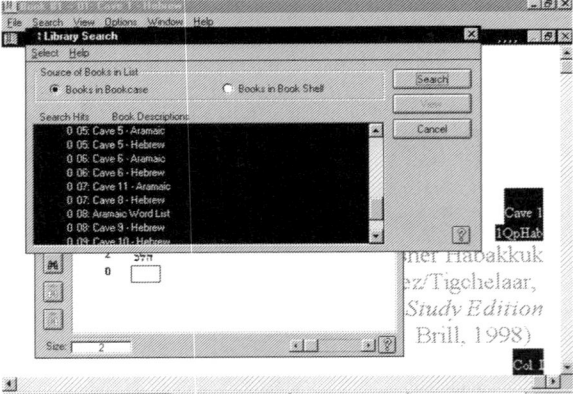

FIGURE 8
Library search window

- Next, select the books in which you wish to perform the search by holding down the control key while clicking on those books (Please note that when the window first opens, all the books may be highlighted).
- *After selecting the books you wish to search, click on the "Search" button.*
That will produce a list showing the number of hits for that word in each of those books which contain that word.
- You may then highlight one of those books and click on the search button to view the list of hits for that book.

V.4 COMPLEX SEARCHES

There are several types of complex searches which may be performed with WordCruncher. Let us begin with the easier ones.

V.4.1 "AND" SEARCHES

These are searches which aim at finding two or more words in proximity to each other, whether contiguous, or merely in the same line.

- Before beginning such a search, look at the drop-down menu called "Space means" in the middle of the SearchManager window.
- From that menu you may choose from several possibilities. If you want to find words which are right beside each other in the text, then choose "exact phrase." If you want words which occur near each other, then you may choose from "within 5 words," "within 10 words," "within 50 words" etc.
- After you have determined the appropriate proximity, you may then type in the words one at a time, separating them by hitting the space bar.

(Please note that prefixes, affixes, articles etc. are counted as separate words.)

Such a search will produce the following results:

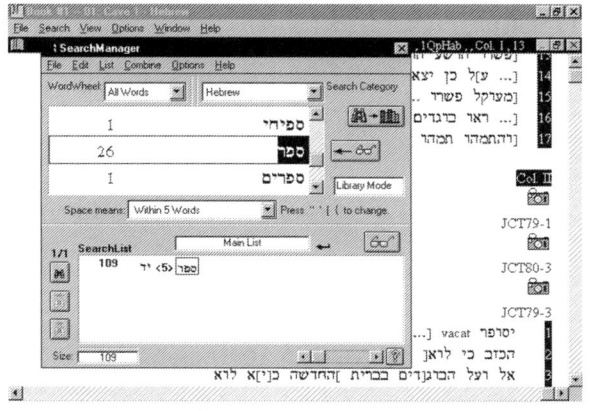

FIGURE 9
SearchManager with an "and" search.

- After that, simply click on the button at the right of the SearchList to produce the list of hits.

V.4.2 "OR" SEARCHES

"Or" searches allow you to find hits on different words which are not grouped together in the same section.

For example, if you wished to find hits on all references to temples within the Hebrew text, you could enter all the various Hebrew words that refer to temples. For the sake of illustration, let us do a search on two of those words, viz. היכל and מקדש.

- First type in היכל
- and then press the "insert" key on your keyboard.
- Then type in מקדש
- and press the insert key again.

That will produce the following window:

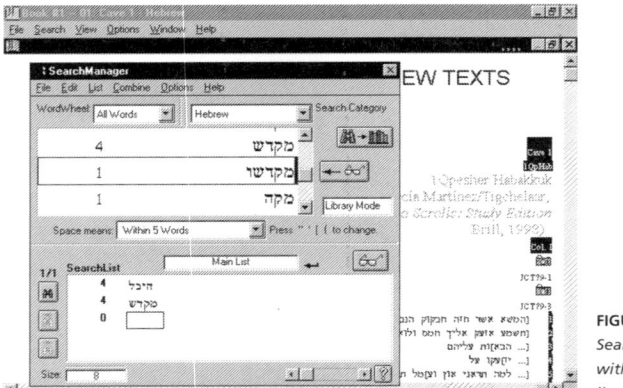

FIGURE 10
*SearchManager
with an "or"
list.*

- Next, you click on the button (with the glasses) to the right of the SearchList and it will produce a list of all occurrences of those two words.

V.4.3 EXACT PHRASES

You can look up an exact phrase by specifying it in the SearchManager.

Example:
- Open the document "Cave 1 – Hebrew"
- and then open the SearchManager using one of the techniques described above.
- Check the "Space means" menu to be sure that "Exact Phrase" is selected.
- Then type in the phrase ועמד כוהן הראש
  Be sure to leave a space between each prefix (*waw* on the first word and the *heh* on the last word in this case) and the main word, because prefixes (i.e. definite article, prepositional prefixes etc.) are treated as separate words in this program. In other words, you will type the following: ו עמד כוהן ה ראש
  (this is the order in which you will type if from right to left, but note that the words will appear from left to right in the window).
- Then push the "insert" button on your keyboard.

That will produce the following window:

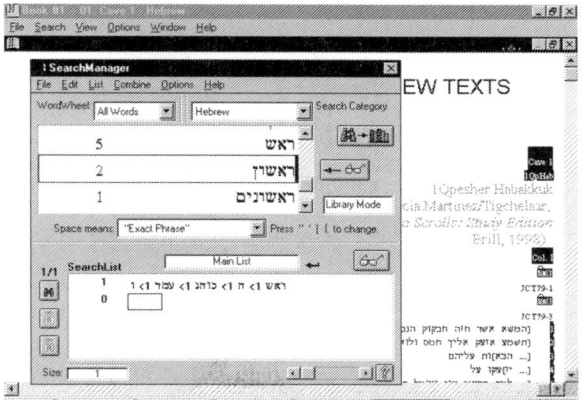

FIGURE 11
SearchManager window with an exact phrase

- Then click on the button at the right of the SearchList to produce the final list of hits, which is a single hit on 1QM, Col. XV, line 4.

V.4.4 WILDCARD SEARCHES

Wildcard searches are particularly useful for scholars who are working on fragments of biblical material and who wish to locate those fragments within the Bible.
- Searches can be done on partial words by opening the "Lists" menu in the SearchManager
- and selecting "substring."
  An asterisk should already be present when the window opens.
- If the search you wish to do involves a wildcard at the beginning of the word, then leave the asterisk in place and type in the letters of the remainder of the word.
- On the other hand, if the wildcard occurs at the end of the word, then backspace to eliminate the asterisk.
- Then type in the initial letters and then add the asterisk and perform the search.

Example:
We will now repeat an actual search that was done for a scholar who had a fragment with the following letters:

]ו א[
]ערב ונ[
]ויה[

- Open the Hebrew Bible
- and then open the SearchManager.

We will ignore the first line, since it does not contain much information.

- So type in ערב
- In the "Space means" menu select "Exact Phrase"
- and then press the space bar
- and type in a *waw* followed by another space.
- Then go to the "List" menu and select "substring."
- In the substring box backspace to eliminate the asterisk,
- type in a nun followed by an asterisk,
- and click on OK.
  This string will be entered in the search list.
  Now we wish to use the words in the last line.
  Until now, we have used the space to mean "exact phrase" because we could see that those first elements followed each other sequentially. But now we cannot be sure how many words intervene between the text on line 2 and that on line 3.
- So go to the "Space means" menu and select "within 25 words."
- Then press the space bar to insert that command into the search list.
- Type in another waw,
- and then go back to the "Space means" menu
- and reselect "Exact phrase" (because we will enter text that immediately follows the waw on the third line).
- Press the space bar again.
- Return to the "List" menu
- and select "Substring."
- Backspace to erase the asterisk
- and type in יה*
- and click on OK.
- Then press "insert"

This will produce the following window:

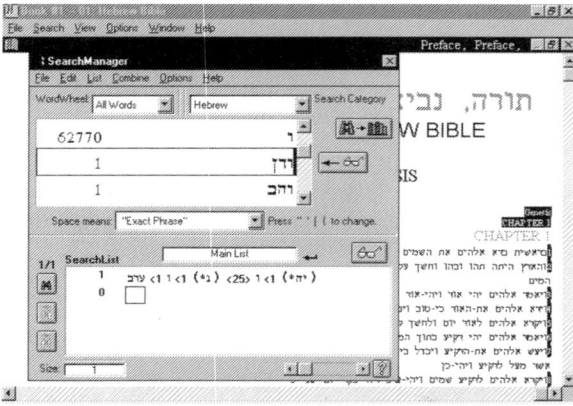

FIGURE 12
Creating a substring list

- and click on the button with the spectacles icon in the lower half of the SearchManager dialog box.

The search results will be displayed and the result should be 1 Samuel 14:24. That is the correct location of the fragment.

V.5 COLLOCATION ANALYSIS

Another valuable feature of WordCruncher software is the ability to do collocation analyses.
- In order to perform this function, you must first generate a "hit list" in the usual fashion.
- Once the results are displayed, open the "View" menu
- and choose "Sort by neighbors."

This will produce a window with the following appearance:

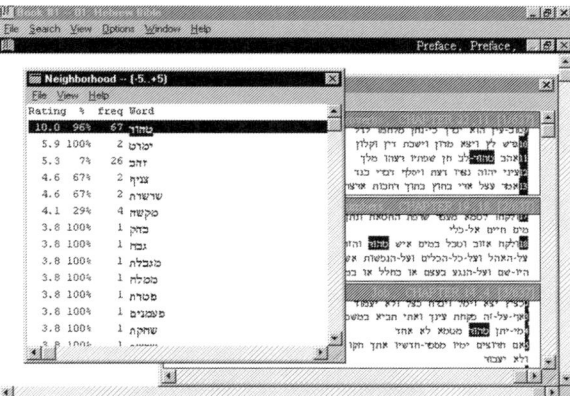

FIGURE 13
Collocation list

The first column shows the "rating." Anything over 2.0 is significant.

The second column shows a % and this refers to the percentage of occurrences of the word in question (listed in the far right column) within 5 words of the target word.

Then there is a column that shows the frequency, i.e. the actual number of times that the word to the right occurs with the target word.

- If you wish a more detailed report (with Z-scores etc.) then open the "View" menu on the "Neighborhood" dialog box
- and choose "detailed report."

This tool can be useful in refining the meanings of words by revealing the usual context in which they are found, and the words with which they are most often associated – either by way of contrast (e.g. "good" and "evil") or by showing words with similar meanings (e.g. "pure" and "holy" – not synonymous, but nevertheless related concepts).

Note:
The collocation range can be modified in the "Neighborhood" dialog box by choosing "Preferences" from the "File" menu.

VI

OUTPUTTING TEXTS

The main purpose of the present DSS Electronic Reference Library is to present the user a comprehensive database with almost all of the Dead Sea Scrolls and to enable him or her to perform searches of various kinds as described above. For that reason, possibilities to export the data to other applications under Windows are limited. Nevertheless, the images can be cut and pasted into other Windows-applications, e.g., Word for Windows. These images can be printed as well, but only in the standard size. The Greek texts can be exported as well, but the user will have to put the encoded text in the GREEK4 font which will be installed automatically with the rest of the program. The present release does not offer a suitable possibility to export the Hebrew and Aramaic texts properly. Exporting these data will result into an encoded text where the letters follow the left-to-right order instead of the required right-to-left order. Nevertheless, the present DSS Electronic Reference Library automatically installs the Frank Ruehl FARMS font which has been used for the Hebrew/Aramaic script, and thus enables the user to use this font for his or her own purposes.

VII

SUGGESTIONS FOR FURTHER IMPROVEMENT

In due course the present release will be followed by an updated, improved and expanded version. Suggestions for improvement in details or procedure may be submitted to the following electronic address:

dss@brill.nl